# The Promise

A story of two sisters, prisoners in a Nazi concentration camp.

*written by* Pnina Bat Zvi and Margie Wolfe
*illustrated by* Isabelle Cardinal

Second Story Press

Rachel pulled herself out of her happy dream. In her sleep she was free to be with her friends and go to school. But now, the gong announced the beginning of another day in Auschwitz prison camp.

Always afraid of what any moment might bring, Rachel inched closer to her older sister in the bunk they shared with four other girls. "Wake up," she whispered in Toby's ear.

"I'm awake," Toby murmured. Her hand automatically reached into her pocket for the tin box. Good. The gold coins were safe.

"Do you still have them?" Rachel whispered as they rose to face whatever danger the day might bring.

"Yes. I promised Mummy, didn't I?"

Toby sighed, remembering how the Nazis had made Rachel work the night they took all the Jewish adults away from their town. Rachel never had a chance to say good-bye to their parents. She wasn't there when their father gave Toby the tin box, saying "This is all we have to leave you. Three gold coins are hidden in the shoe paste. Use them only if you have to."

And Rachel hadn't seen how her mother pulled Toby close. "Use the gold for something important," she said. "You will know when the time is right. And above all, stay together. This is how you will both survive."

Two years had passed since that terrible night. Their parents were never seen again.

Both girls jumped as the door to Barrack 25 banged open.

"*Achtung!* Attention!" the Nazi guard shouted. "Line up in the yard!" The German shepherd by her side snarled—always alert and ready to lunge at anyone.

Once outside, the girls stepped forward as a prisoner called the roll and checked off their names.

"Sofie?"

"Present!"

"Eva?"

"Present!"

"Rachel?"

"Present!"

"Lola?"

Silence.

"Lola? Lo—"

"Cross her off the list! She is gone," the guard hissed. Someone in line sobbed and the guard yelled, "Stop whining, stupid girl!"

Lola had been too sick to work the day before and had stayed in bed. When the others returned later, she had disappeared. They all knew Lola would not be back. Her friend, Pessa, wept herself to sleep.

*Please, don't let us get sick*, Toby prayed, looking over at Rachel.

"Toby!"

The sound of her name startled the girl back to attention. She stepped forward. "Present!"

One day the prisoners built a wall of heavy fieldstones, the next they took it apart, the next they built it again. No one was brave enough to question such foolishness.

Toby resisted in her own way. When the guards weren't watching, she'd stop working and stare defiantly at them. When they turned back, she'd quickly pick up a rock, as if she had never stopped. Toby risked being caught and punished, but the risk was worth it to her.

Eva thought she was fearless. Pessa thought she was reckless. But Rachel knew her sister best. This act of defiance was Toby's small victory over those who had taken away their parents and their freedom and made them into slaves, simply because they were Jewish.

Today the guards were nastier than usual. "Hurry! No talking! Move faster!" ordered one.

Rachel turned to check on her sister and almost cried out. There, lying on the ground in plain view, was the tin of gold coins!

What should Rachel do? She couldn't reach for the tin without being seen. Toby hadn't noticed and was passing another rock to Eva. And now one of the guards was coming closer with his dog. The animal was sure to sniff at it.

She must act. Toby had looked after the coins for two years. Now it was up to her.

Rachel pretended to stumble sideways and dropped the big stone she was holding on top of the tin, covering it.

"Clumsy girl! Get back to work!" the guard yelled. His dog crouched low.

"I'm sorry! It won't happen again," Rachel apologized. She stooped to pick up the rock, making certain she lifted the box along with it.

After the guard left, Rachel changed places with Eva so she could be next to her sister.

"Are you okay?" Toby asked, concerned.

Rachel nodded. "I have the shoe paste tin in my hand. Take it."

Toby felt her pocket. Empty! She made sure no one was looking and then slid the box from Rachel's palm to her own. Pretending to wipe dirt from her hands, she slipped the tin back where it belonged.

That night the girls lay on their bunk, waiting to escape into sleep.

"I was so proud of you today," Toby murmured. "Mummy and Daddy would be, too."

Rachel was surprised by the praise. "I'm not nearly as courageous as you. I worry that I won't be able to keep our promise if a Nazi soldier tries to separate us."

Toby shook her head. "Don't be fooled. I'm not as brave as you think. I just act stronger than I feel, and I convince myself that I'm brave." She kissed her sister's cheek. "But one thing I know. This insanity can't last forever. What we must do is survive until this war ends. Rest now, Rachel. You saved us today."

The next morning was cold and rainy. The prisoners worked taking apart the wall they had built the day before. Their teeth chattered on the march back to camp. Most of them warmed up after a while, but by nighttime, Rachel was still shivering.

The girls tried to help. Sofie gave Rachel her dinner soup. Pessa covered her with her own flimsy blanket. Eva rubbed her ice-cold hands. Toby held her close, trying to calm the shaking, as Rachel fell asleep in her arms.

Everyone remembered how Lola had disappeared. Rachel needed to be well for morning roll call. The Nazis didn't keep those who were too weak to work.

But by dawn Rachel was no better.

"I hurt all over. Let me sleep a little longer," she pleaded.

"You can't!" Toby urged. "I'll do your share of work today, if you just get up."

But Rachel couldn't. Hunger and hard labor had taken their toll. So, when Rachel's name was called that morning, Toby stepped forward, trying to control the tremor in her voice. "My sister has a cold today—nothing serious. Tomorrow she will be better."

The guard signaled the prisoner to erase Rachel's name from the list. Toby's knees buckled. She begged to stay with Rachel and do a double shift the next day, but the guard ignored her.

For the first time since coming to Auschwitz, the sisters were separated.

Toby worked feverishly all day with no thought of defying the guards. Frantic with worry, she couldn't wait to get back to the barrack. But on her return, just as she feared, their bunk was empty.

"They took Rachel!" she cried. "I have to find her before it's too late!"

"It *is* too late," Pessa said softly. "Don't make trouble, or you will disappear as well."

"There's nothing to be done," Sofie spoke gently. "She's gone."

"You are a prisoner yourself. What can you do?" asked Eva.

Toby listened to the girls but couldn't accept what they were saying. "You may be right," she said, "but I'm going to find her. She's my sister." The others could hear the determination in her voice.

A plan began to form in Toby's head. *I still have the coins,* she thought. "Quick, Eva, give me your scarf. Rachel might need it to hide her face."

Eva handed her a scarf and so did Pessa. "You may need one yourself," she said. "Rachel's probably in Barrack Number 29. That's where they keep sick people until—"

Eva cut her off. "Be careful. Rachel admired your bravery, but thought you took too many chances. She worried about you."

Tears stung Toby's eyes. At home she had treated Rachel like an annoying little pest, always tagging along. Now, she would do anything to save her sister. "Pray for us," she said. As Toby moved toward the door she thought, *If I'm caught this will be the last time I see these friends.*

In Barrack 29, Rachel was losing hope.

"We are all in such danger here," she had whispered to an old woman beside her. "Do you think help will come?" They were watching the barrack guard write a list as she strolled between the beds of sick prisoners.

The elderly woman answered her gently. "There is no help for anyone in Auschwitz." Then, seeing how her words had frightened the girl, she added, "I suppose miracles do happen…sometimes."

Trying to avoid the guard's attention, Rachel had found a place to cry alone. She pictured her sister's face. Would Toby survive without her? They *did* need a miracle. All the prisoners in Auschwitz did. But it seemed the world had forgotten them.

Reaching toward the sandy ground, Rachel scratched the letters T-O-B-Y with her finger.

Outside, the guard was just leaving Barrack 29. Toby darted behind a storage shed, but the German shepherd saw her and strained at its leash. Impatient for supper, the guard yanked her dog forward and passed within inches. Toby collapsed against the wall, terrified.

When her heart slowed, she peeked around the corner. An inmate—a prisoner who hoped to survive by helping the Nazis—was now guarding Barrack 29. Toby recognized her. Perhaps this was a bit of good luck. She scurried forward.

"My sister is inside," Toby whispered. "Please, let me in."

"Impossible," the guard hissed, looking away.

Toby knew what she must do. "I'll give you a gold coin if you help me."

The guard's eyes shifted slightly. "It's too dangerous."

"*Two* coins, then. *Please!* We only have each other."

"Come!" The woman pulled Toby inside.

Toby took the tin from her pocket and dug out two coins. The guard snatched them and rubbed away the shoe paste until the gold glimmered. Satisfied, she pocketed them. "Hurry!" she ordered.

Toby searched frantically, but couldn't find Rachel. She rushed back to the guard. "Did they already take my sister?"

The guard shrugged.

"I'll check again."

"No! Make my risk worthwhile."

Toby removed the last coin. "Here!" she said. "It's all I have. There is no more."

This time Toby was extra careful. She noticed a doorway and peered through it. There was her sister in a small fenced-in area behind the barrack.

Toby cried out and ran to embrace Rachel. "We have to get away. Come with me. Now!"

The girls ran toward the waiting guard.

"Be quiet, or we will all be shot!" the woman hissed.

Toby handed Eva's scarf to her sister. "Put it on."

Breathless and shaking, the two girls slipped out into the gloom.

"How did y—"

"Shh," Toby cut her off. "*Come on!*"


In Barrack 25, the girls were greeted with hugs, tears of joy, and lots of questions.

"You risked everything for me," Rachel said.

"You are my pesky little sister. What else was I supposed to do!"

Rachel smiled. "And you are the bossy miracle I needed."

For that one single night the prisoners of Barrack 25 forgot to be afraid.

No one wanted to think about what would happen when the sun rose.

When the roll call ended that morning, every girl except one had stepped forward at the sound of her name. The guard looked at Rachel, astonished.

"You are not supposed to be here. How did you get back?" she demanded.

Toby spoke up. "I took her out of Barrack 29." As the guard and her dog moved forward, Toby added, "I had to! I promised my parents we would stay together!"

"Blame me!" Rachel cried. "I was sick. My sister was trying to protect me."

The guard pointed at Toby. "Move out of line and unbutton your dress. Face the wall!" She bent to unhook the dog and ordered it to stay. No one made a sound until the guard began whipping Toby's bare back with the leash.

Rachel cried out for the guard to stop, but she continued.

When it was finally over, Toby fell to the ground, and Rachel rushed to her side.

The guard clipped the leash to the dog's collar. "I've done my job," she told Toby. "You have been punished." Then, to everyone's amazement, she turned to the prisoner at her side. "Put Rachel's name back on the list. She can stay with her sister."

Shouts of relief filled the air as the guard marched away. Toby and Rachel stared after her in disbelief. Was it possible that their love for each other had touched the heart of a Nazi guard? They would never know.

The scars on Toby's back remained for a long time. But when the Nazis were finally defeated, and the surviving prisoners were freed, Rachel and Toby left the camp, hand in hand, carrying an empty shoe paste tin. The coins were gone.

But the promise had been kept.

# Epilogue

Toby (right) and Rachel (left) remained devoted sisters and best friends for the next fifty years. Even when distance separated them, their hearts and spirits were always together. They remained forever friends with those girls from Barrack 25 who also survived.

The authors, who are close cousins, wrote this story as told to them by their mothers.

*To my courageous sons, Michael and Ilay*
*—P.B.Z.*

*To the memory of my parents, Toby and Joseph,*
*and the grandparents I never knew.*
*—M.W.*

*To my parents, Claude and Edyth, and my sister, Nathalie.*
*I am so grateful for the unending support and love we share.*
*Family is the most precious thing in the world.*
*—I.C.*

---

*I would like to thank my sister, Bilha, for remembering the stories that our mother and aunt told over the years at the kitchen table. Also, I appreciate the support of family members, Beni, Yehudi, and Nili when I thought my own memories were slipping away.*
*—P.B.Z.*

*Thank you, Pnina, for recognizing that we could honor our mothers by writing this book. And love to my sister, Helen, for remembering with me.*
*We both know that we could not have done this without our editor Kathryn Cole and the other women at Second Story Press—Allie Chenoweth, Emma Rodgers, Melissa Kaita, Phuong Truong, Ellie Sipila, and Natasha Bozorgi. Isabelle Cardinal's images perfectly interpret the mood of the text. Also, thank you to Martin Baranek, who described the daily routines in Auschwitz to us.*
*—M.W.*

---

Library and Archives Canada Cataloguing in Publication

Bat-Zvi, Pnina, author
The promise / Pnina Bat Zvi and Margie Wolfe ; illustrated by Isabelle Cardinal.

ISBN 978-1-77260-058-2 (hardcover)

1. Jewish children in the Holocaust--Biography--Juvenile literature.
2. Auschwitz (Concentration camp)--Juvenile literature.  3. Holocaust, Jewish (1939-1945)--Juvenile literature.  I. Wolfe, Margie, 1949-, author II. Cardinal, Isabelle, 1969-, illustrator  III. Title.

D804.48.B37 2018          j940.53'1853862          C2017-906248-4

*Second Story Press gratefully acknowledges the support of the Ontario Arts Council and the Canada Council for the Arts for our publishing program. We acknowledge the financial support of the Government of Canada through the Canada Book Fund.*

Published by
Second Story Press
20 Maud Street, Suite 401
Toronto, Ontario, Canada
M5V 2M5
www.secondstorypress.ca